THE BEACHCOMBER'S BOOK

The Beachcomber's Book

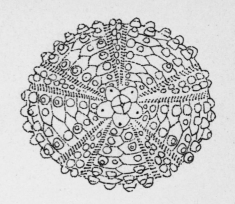

By Bernice Kohn

Illustrated by Arabelle Wheatley

THE VIKING PRESS   NEW YORK

574.9 Seashore life
745.5 Crafts

SBN 670–05052–0

1   2   3   4   5   75   74   73   72   71

Contents

What Is a Beachcomber?

Do you love to walk along the edge of the sea, looking down more often than up? Do you have to pick up pretty shells, pebbles, and other sea-tossed objects? Do you usually take along a bag full of beach "pickings" when it's time to go home? If so, then you are a beginning beachcomber. If you can use the things you take home, you are a real genuine bona fide beachcomber.

This book will give you some ideas about how to use the things you find on the beach. More important, it will help you to use your imagination to make things that no one has ever made before.

The all-around beachcomber knows how to collect and how to create. Best of all, he knows how to *see* what is on the beach. He notices things that ordinary people pass by. The beach, in any weather or any season, is a place of endless excitement and adventure. The beach-comber explores and enjoys every bit of it. In time, he may expand his beachcombing activities to become a serious collector, an artist, or a scientist.

This book begins with things that are plentiful and easy to find—sand, pebbles, shells, seaweed. It goes on to things that you really have to look for, such as beach glass, driftwood, and found objects. It ends with shellfish cookery and seaside gardens.

Do all of the projects or just some of them, and you will never be the same on a beach again. The beach will become a world unlike any other, and your pleasure in it will grow and grow. Try it and see.

Happy beachcombing!

The Sandy Beach

What is the first word you think of when someone says "beach"? If you are like many people, the word is "sand." Sand, because on most beaches there's so much of it. You can walk on it, roll in it, dig in it, sleep on it. It gets between your toes, in your ears, in your hair—and, too often, even in your mouth.

Just because sand is so plentiful, you probably don't pay much attention to it. If you stop to think about it, sand is more interesting than it looks. All sand is really rock that has been ground down by the action of the water. The kind of rock on the particular shore accounts for the kind of sand on the beach. The most common sand in the United States is gray. It is made up of quartz and other minerals. There is also white coral sand in Florida, white gypsum sand in New Mexico, green olivine sand in Hawaii. In other countries, you can find beaches that are red, black, or pink.

No matter what color the sand is, most beachcombers don't take it home (except in their shoes). But if you are willing to lug home a whole bagful, there really are things you can use it for. For example, you can make sand lanterns.

SAND LANTERNS

You will need: **Large brown paper bags from the supermarket**
Sand
Candles

Open each bag all the way and turn down a six-inch cuff at the top. Now put about six inches of sand into every bag and stick a candle firmly in the center of the sand. Be sure that the candle is well away from the sides of the bag and anchored in the sand so it cannot tip.

When you light the lanterns at dusk, you will see that the bags act as lamp shades and provide a soft glowing light. The lanterns are perfect for an evening party or for a dinner served outside. Scatter them around the garden, use them in rows along the walk or around the edges of a patio.

And then there is sand painting. This is an ancient American art. Indian paintings were made by sprinkling sand on the ground. The Navaho Indians were expert sand painters and used the paintings in some of their ceremonies. After the ceremony, the paintings were destroyed or simply swept away by the wind.

You can make sand paintings that are permanent, and if you want to, you can frame them.

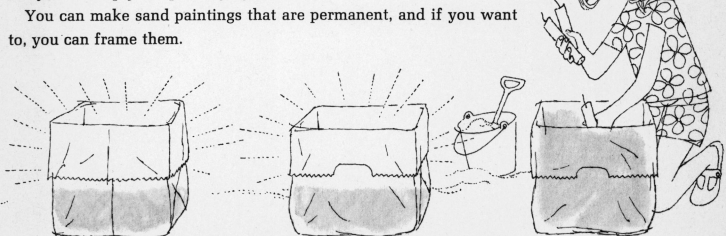

SAND PAINTING

You will need: **Sand of two colors (look for streaks of red garnet or other contrasting sand on your beach)**

OR sand and shells of a different color from the sand. Crush the shells into small particles.

Cardboard (a shirt cardboard is good)

All-purpose white glue (not paste)

A small watercolor brush

A pencil

A shell or a paper cup for mixing glue

Optional: a frame and scissors

If you plan to frame your painting, cut your cardboard to fit the frame before you begin.

Draw a design lightly with pencil on the cardboard. Keep it simple. Try not to have many small details. Decide how you will use your two colors as you go.

Mix some glue with an equal amount of water. This will make it easy to spread and will also make it dry clear instead of white.

Paint one small area of the drawing with glue and sprinkle sand on it. Shake off the extra sand and paint glue on the next portion. Con-

tinue until you have done all the parts on which you want to use the first color.

Wait a few minutes until the glue has begun to dry, and then fill in the remaining portions with the other color.

There will be some bare patches here and there. Fill them in with a drop of glue and add sand. Let the painting dry overnight, then put it in the frame. If you don't want to frame it, cover it with clear plastic wrap and glue a paper clip to the back for a hanger.

You can have a really exciting experience with sand if you ever see "Cold Fire on the Night Beach." There are no exact directions for this one. It is purely a matter of luck—of being in the right place at the right time.

In the sea there are many tiny organisms that produce the same kind of cold light that fireflies do. In the tropics, it is well known that the water and beach often "light up"; but most people don't know that it happens in temperate climates, too.

One night in early spring, my husband and I took a walk along the beach at East Hampton, near the tip of New York's Long Island. We walked in the wet sand at the water's edge, and I lagged behind for a moment. I was astonished to see showers of bright sparks shooting up from my husband's heels every time he took a step.

I called to him, and as he turned around, the sand under his feet glowed with light. Then we began to experiment. Rubbing the wet sand with our sneakers or fingers made flares of light. Swirling our hands in the water was even more spectacular—and when we held up our hands, the drops of water that fell from our fingers sparkled.

Later we noticed that whenever a fish swam through the water there was a glow. And when we threw stones into the sea, they made little fountains of light.

There are no exact directions for finding light-producing organisms. Every book I have read on the subject says that they *may* occur on Long Island in the late summer, but I saw them in the early spring. So if you are on the beach in the dark, rub some wet sand or stir up the water. You never can tell!

The Pebbly Beach

Pebbles are pieces of rock that are on their way to becoming sand. Broken off from the large rock mass, beaten and battered by waves and currents, polished against each other, beach pebbles have no rough edges. Often they are as smooth as eggs.

If you have been to a pebbly beach, you were probably charmed by the colors of the wet pebbles along the water's edge. Red, gold, green, white, black—all shiny as gems. You gathered up a batch of the prettiest ones and took them home, but the next day they were just stones. All the beauty was gone. No shine, no sparkle, hardly any color. What happened?

Since pebbles are constantly being ground, they are covered with tiny scratches. Rub a shiny marble with sandpaper and see how dull

it gets. Put the pebbles—or the marble—in water and they glisten. When they dry, they are dull and drab.

But there is a way to keep beach pebbles beautiful, just as they were when you found them. When you get your pebbles home, wash them in fresh water and dry them. Then rub each pebble with a drop or two of mineral oil or baby oil. Do not use cooking oil, as it turns sticky after a while.

Small, colorful pebbles make a charming centerpiece for the table when they are placed in a glass bowl, with or without water.

Use smooth pebbles of similar size to cover the soil in a flowerpot. If you use all black or all white pebbles, they will look faintly Japanese. The pebbles are attractive and they serve a practical purpose, too, since they keep the soil from drying out so fast.

Tiny pebbles of different colors can also make a lovely mosaic.

MOSAIC

You will need: **Small pebbles, a handful of each of several colors**
A piece of board, driftwood if you can find it
Two small eyehooks
A piece of picture wire or string
Clear household cement (such as Duco)
A pencil

Put the eyehooks into the back of the board so that you will be able to hang it. Place them exactly across from each other, a little above the center and about an inch in from each side.

Draw the design on the front of the board with pencil. You can apply the cement right from the tube, but do only a small area at a time since it dries very quickly. Drop enough pebbles onto the wet glue to cover it and go on to the next portion.

When the mosaic is finished and thoroughly dry, fasten the wire

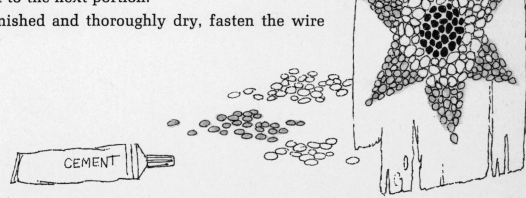

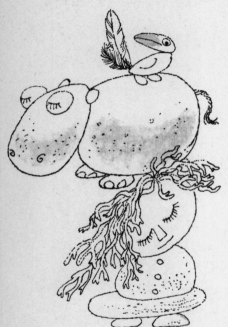

or string between the eyehooks and hang up your creation for all to admire.

Larger, water-smooth pebbles are fine for making pebble sculptures.

PEBBLE SCULPTURE

You will need: **Pebbles in a variety of shapes and sizes, washed and dried**
Clear-drying epoxy cement
A felt-tipped pen with waterproof ink
Odd materials such as string, yarn, bits of pipe cleaner, seaweed, shells, or anything else you have handy
A toothpick or matchstick
Clear household cement

Epoxy cement usually comes in two little tubes, and you have to mix equal parts from each tube. Mix with a toothpick or a matchstick on a scrap of cardboard.

Use your imagination to create people or animals. Very often the shape of the stones will suggest what you should make. A round flattish stone may make you think of a turtle. A great big fat stone may suggest a hippopotamus, while another might look like a bird.

Before you use any cement, put your sculpture together to see how it looks. Use a flat-bottomed stone for the base so that it sits solidly. The whole thing should stay together by itself so that it doesn't topple over before the glue dries. With a little patience (and a large stock of stones), you will find that this is possible. If there is one pebble that is so perfect that you *must* use it and it absolutely won't stay put, figure out a way to prop it against the wall or a pile of books to keep it in place. Epoxy glue is very strong and will hold even large rocks when it is thoroughly dry.

When your sculpture is glued together, let it dry overnight without moving it. The next day, paint on eyes, nose, mouth, and other details with the felt pen. Use bits of string, yarn, seaweed, and other odds and ends to add finishing touches such as hair, tail, or whiskers. These can be put on with clear household cement, which dries quickly.

Of course, you don't have to make people and animals. You can use beach pebbles to make abstract sculptures. Heavy ones, with a flat stone on the bottom and a piece of felt glued underneath, make splendid bookends.

Seashells on the Seashore

Every beachcomber, East or West, is familiar with clam shells, scallop shells, jingle shells, and boat shells. But it is a rare person indeed who can name all (or most) of the shells on any one beach.

The exception is a shell collector. Shell collecting is a popular hobby. Collectors swap shells with each other. Some collectors sell their collections to museums. Others run shell shops or may sell to such shops.

The dyed-in-the-wool beachcomber would much rather find a shell than buy it. The thrill of finding a rare specimen on the beach could never be matched by finding it in a shop. And one of the joys of a collection is remembering when and where you found each shell.

As with stamps or coins or anything else that people collect, if you want your specimens to have real value, there are a few rules you have to follow.

As you know, a seashell is the covering of a live animal. The empty shells that are cast up on the beach are called dead shells. Any shell that has been on the beach for a long time becomes faded and worn. The very best shells are those that are taken alive. Almost as good are those that are found freshly dead.

The beaches of bays are often richer in shells than ocean beaches, but this depends on local conditions. On all beaches, the best time to look for shells is at low tide. Shells are cast up by the high water and remain near the high-tide line until the water comes back to wash them out to sea again. A low tide right after a storm or a hurricane is the best shelling time of all.

Collect your shells in a plastic pail or bag. Metal may leave rust marks. Look under rocks, near piers and pilings, in mud flats and tidal pools. A paddle board with a window in it is valuable for hunting shells in shallow water. Without it, light reflections on the surface of the water often make it hard to see the bottom.

Dead shells found on a sandy beach may need no cleaning besides rinsing in fresh water. On the other hand, they may be covered with stains which won't wash off. Shells from a muddy beach are almost sure to need special cleaning.

Clean such shells as well as you can with an old toothbrush. If stubborn stains remain, mix one cup of liquid laundry bleach into a pail of water. Soak the shells for a few hours, overnight if necessary. Don't leave them in the solution any longer than you have to because the colors may become bleached.

So much for dead shells. Live ones are more complicated. There is hardly a beachcomber anywhere who, at least once, has not taken home a beautifully curved "empty" whelk shell—only to be greeted by one of the worst smells imaginable a few days later.

Hinged shells (or *bivalves*—clams, scallops, and the like) are easy to deal with. You can see at once whether they are empty or not.

bivalve shells

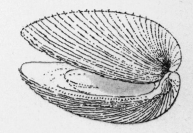

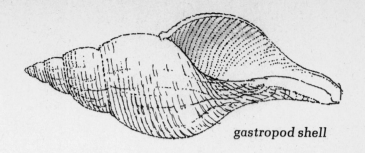

gastropod shell

But how can you tell when there is an animal, or part of an animal, in the bottom of a spiral *(gastropod)* shell? You can't! So play it safe.

Place live and doubtful shells in a pot of water and heat on the stove very, very slowly. A sudden hot-water bath makes shells dull.

As soon as the water comes to a boil, lift out the shells with a spoon and spread them to cool. When you can handle them, take one shell at a time and carefully dig out the animal with a pointed instrument. Use bent wire, a nutpick, a hairpin, whatever you can find to fit into the shell. Work slowly and try to get out the entire animal without breaking it off. If you leave a piece in the bottom of the shell, you have a problem.

You can solve it by soaking the shell in alcohol for a couple of hours and drying it in the shade. This will not remove the remains, but it will make them "smell-proof."

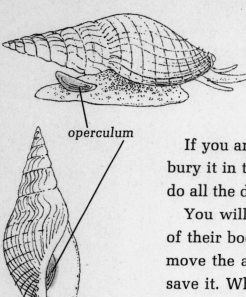

operculum

If you aren't in a hurry, the easiest way of all to clean a shell is to bury it in the garden. Leave it there for a few days and the ants will do all the dirty work.

You will notice that gastropods have a disk on the outward ends of their bodies. It forms a "door" to seal up the shell. When you remove the animal, cut off this disk (the *operculum*) with a knife and save it. When your shell is clean and dry, glue the operculum back into place. It is easier to do if you stuff the shell with cotton first.

If your shells have lost any of their luster, rub them with a drop of mineral oil. And now you are ready for labels.

Most shells have common names, but these names differ from place to place. What you call a boat shell may be known as a slipper shell elsewhere. Jingle shells on some beaches are called sailor's toenails on others. Avoid mix-ups by labeling each shell with its scientific name.

You can find shell handbooks in every library, and they will give you the information you need. Look for your shell in the book by its common name or by its picture. Read the description carefully to make sure you have the right one. Check the size, the color, and the markings. Check the geographical range, too. If you found your shell in Maine and the book says that it is found from southern California to central Mexico, you probably have the wrong shell.

You will notice that the shells in the book have scientific names like *Anomia simplex,* Orbigny (jingle shell). The first name, always spelled with a capital letter, is the name of the *genus,* the group of animals to which the specimen belongs. The second name, spelled with a small letter, is the *species* name. This describes that particular animal. If there is still another name (in this case, Orbigny), it is the name of the scientist who first described the species. When there is a common name (such as jingle shell), it is usually given also.

To make your label, follow the same system. Put on the full scientific name and the common name. Add the date, indicate where you found the shell, and include any other information you might like to have. For example, you could say "off the south side of Wilson's pier" or "day after northeaster" or "buried in three inches of mud."

Store your collection in egg cartons, matchboxes, or any other containers that you find handy. Always keep your shells out of the sunlight so that they won't fade.

47 *Anomia simplex*
(jingle shell)
august 14 197?
East Hampton L.I. N.Y.

How to Be a Shell Artist

You may not be a collector at heart. Not everyone is. Perhaps you would rather make things with the shells you find. And, of course, there is nothing to stop you from being collector and artist both.

Shells have a long history of usage. American Indians used shells for money. So did people in several African cultures. Young girls wore strings of cowrie-shell beads to show their wealth. You might say that these were a "cowrie dowry."

Shells aren't used for money any more, but shell beads are still attractive and fun to make. Use any small shells that are plentiful on your beach. Some shells already have holes in them. If yours do not, test one to see if you can make a hole without shattering the shell.

Place the shell on a board and hold a nail where you want the hole.

One light tap with a hammer should do it for most shells. The beads in the picture are jingle shells—or *Anomia simplex*, Orbigny—and they were found on the Atlantic coast. The Pacific coast has jingle shells, too, but they are a slightly different variety, *Anomia peruviana*.

The jingle shells pictured lie flat because each has two holes, side by side, and the string is threaded through both of them. You can see from the pictures some different kinds of beads you can make by using different kinds of shells and different ways of stringing them. You can also use shells of several sizes, or small shells at the ends with large ones in the center. Or you can alternate two kinds of shells or separate shells with dried seeds or berries. Your design will be inspired by the materials you have at hand.

To string shells, use a string that is strong but not too thick. Dental floss is excellent for beads. So is nylon bead cord, available in most five-and-tens. If you use ordinary string or heavy-duty thread, make the end stiff by dipping it in household cement and letting it dry.

You can use strings of shells, too, to make an attractive and musical decoration for your home.

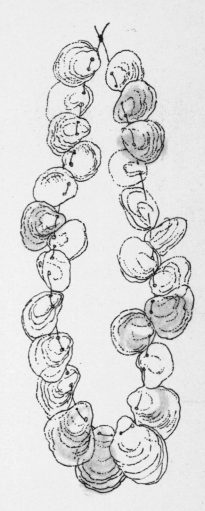

WIND CHIME

You will need: **Many small shells**
String
A hanger such as a small basket, a piece of
driftwood, or anything else that you like

String shells as you would for beads, but make each string only about six inches long. Fasten the end of each string to your hanger. The wind chime in the picture is made from a small basket and jingle shells. Jingle shells are especially good for a chime because they make such a lovely jingly sound. If you don't want the shells to bunch up, tie a knot under each shell, and it will stay put. A wind chime should be hung from the ceiling or in a doorway where there is a breeze. Hang your chime in your beach house or on a porch or patio, and you will always hear the wind blow.

Has there ever been a beach cottage anywhere that didn't contain half a dozen large clam shells for all sorts of purposes? They are used for ash trays, candy dishes, spoon rests on the stove, bobby-pin and jewelry catchalls, soap dishes, and dozens of other things.

You can dress up a plain shell for your own house or to give as a gift.

SHELL FLOWER

You will need: **A large clam shell**
Some small shells
An old plate (or a piece of glass)
Clear household cement
A small paring knife
Nail polish remover

Squeeze a small blob of cement onto the plate. Select four or five small shells of the same size and kind. Arrange them in the cement so that their edges overlap a bit and there is a little hole left in the center. With the tip of the knife, press down on each shell at the center so that the outer edges stick up. When the flower is arranged to your taste, leave it alone for a few minutes until the cement begins to set. Now carefully pass the blade of the knife under the flower to separate it from the plate. Don't worry if the flower gets pushed out of shape (it will!) because there is still time to fix it.

Put a dab of cement on the hinge part of your big clam shell and lift

the flower onto it with the knife blade. Now rearrange the flower so that it is just the way you want it. Add a center, using a tiny snail shell, a pebble, or anything else that you like. Let the shell flower dry for several hours. In the meantime, you can clean up the plate, the knife, and your hands with nail polish remover.

With a little practice, you will find that you can make dogwood blossoms, daffodils, roses, and many other flowers. Instead of using them all on clam shells, you can cement safety pins to the backs and make pins. Or buy earring backs in the five-and-ten and glue two identical flowers onto a pair of them.

You can use shells to make animals and birds, too. Use your local shells and your imagination.

Glue shells to a large piece of driftwood to make a collage or assemblage. Use tiny shells to make a mosaic. Pile shells into a brandy snifter or an apothecary jar for a centerpiece. Glue shells around the base of a dime-store candleholder. Completely cover a trinket box. Glue shell decorations on stiff paper to make greeting cards or gift tags. Use a large gastropod shell to hold flowers.

Or you might try making a mobile.

A MOBILE

You will need: **Two pieces of stiff straight wire (from a hanger, an orange crate, etc.)**

A piece of sticky tape (adhesive, mending, or electrical tape)

Heavy-duty thread (white or clear nylon is best as it is least visible)

Thumbtack

Shells of different sizes

Scissors

A toothpick

Clear household cement

Join the wires together with tape to form a cross. Bend the ends gently downward. Tie a long piece of heavy-duty thread around the joint and hang up the frame. It is easiest to work with when it hangs freely, so hang it at shoulder height from a thumbtack in a doorway—or from the underside of a table if you don't mind sitting on the floor.

Thread your shells, using large shells and small ones, single shells

and strings of them, long threads and short threads. Follow the directions on pages 32-33 for making holes in the shells and stringing them.

Now tie a threaded shell on the end of one of the arms. As soon as you do this, the mobile will tip to one side. Balance it by tying another shell to the opposite end of the same arm. Then attach shells to each end of the other arm. Continue to add shells in this fashion along the length of the arms as well as at the ends, using long and short threads, single shells and strings of them. If you add a particularly heavy shell, balance it by placing another heavy one on the opposite end.

When you have tied on all your shells, your mobile probably will not be quite balanced. To get it just right, experiment with each thread by sliding it toward the center or away from it until the mobile

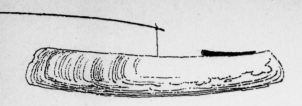

hangs level and you like the design. It takes some patience—but it's worth it. Finally, with a toothpick, apply a drop of clear household cement to each knot. This will help prevent the threads from sliding and unbalancing your mobile in a breeze.

After you have tried this mobile, you may want to go on to more difficult ones, such as the mobile on page 48, using three or four pieces of wire, or driftwood sticks instead of the wire. The directions for balancing are the same, but for this type of mobile you must work from the bottom up, balancing the shells on each arm before attaching it to the one above. You can find books showing how to make all kinds of mobiles in your local library.

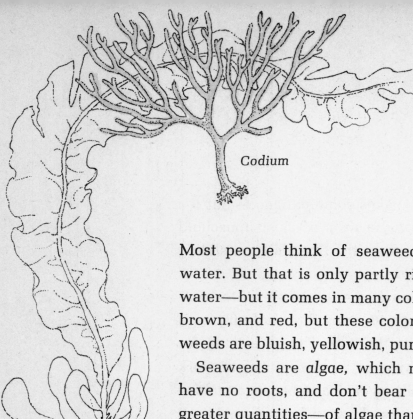

Codium

Alaria

Seaweed

Most people think of seaweed as green plants that grow in the water. But that is only partly right. True enough, seaweed grows in water—but it comes in many colors. The main color groups are green, brown, and red, but these colors are often mixed, so that some seaweeds are bluish, yellowish, purple, and other shades.

Seaweeds are *algae*, which means that they contain chlorophyll, have no roots, and don't bear flowers. There are more kinds—and greater quantities—of algae than you can imagine. Many are so small that they can only be seen with a microscope. But the most familiar kind is seaweed.

Because seaweed is easily found on almost every beach, it has many enthusiastic collectors. Look for seaweeds on incoming waves, at the high-tide line, around the roots of grasses at the water's edge, on rocks or pilings. You will notice that some seaweeds are free floating, while others attach themselves firmly to some solid object with a *holdfast.* The holdfast looks like one or more tiny rubber suction cups. It is not a root but acts as an anchor. Whenever you remove a seaweed from a rock or a shell, try to preserve the holdfast. You may have to use a knife to loosen it.

Collect only perfect specimens that are not too large to handle. Wash them well in sea water to remove sand and put them into a pail with some of the water.

When you go home, take some extra sea water with you if you can. If it is too much to carry and you must use fresh water to prepare your specimens, take care not to leave them in for more than a few minutes. Fresh water spoils the color of many seaweeds.

Pick out one specimen and float it in a shallow basin of water. If it is very large or if it has ragged spots, trim it with scissors. Just be sure to leave a typical section that will show how the plant grows.

Now slide a sheet of stiff paper (or two sheets of unlined notebook paper or typewriter paper) under the seaweed and lift it clear of the

sea water

water. Tilt the paper a bit to drain it. Gently rearrange any frond that is out of place.

Put the wet paper on a large sheet of blotting paper if you have one. If you haven't, use several layers of newspapers instead. Cover the specimen with a clean cloth, such as a piece of old sheet, and put more blotting paper on top of the cloth. When you prepare a second specimen, put it right on top of the first, cover it with cloth, and continue in the same way. When you are all finished, put a board on top of the pile and weigh it down with a couple of books.

Change the blotters and cloths once a day for two or three days. Continue to press the seaweeds until they are completely dry.

You may find that some seaweeds are too bulky to be stacked in a pile with others. These must be pressed separately.

Also, some seaweeds are very slimy, full of a gelatin-like substance. These should be hung up by a string until they are partly dry and then pressed on white typing paper between newspapers.

When your specimens have dried, you will find that many of them have glued themselves to the paper on which they were spread. Those that haven't can be fastened with a drop or two of rubber cement or other glue. Mount the sheets in a large loose-leaf notebook or scrapbook.

Directions for labeling seaweed are exactly the same as for shells. Get a handbook from your library for the scientific names. Common sea lettuce would be labeled *Ulva lactuca* (sea lettuce). You may want to add a note on where you found it.

With so many tons of seaweed in the world, only a very tiny portion of it ever finds its way into collections. In nature it provides both food and shelter for countless fish, shellfish, and other creatures. But man has found many uses for it, too.

Coastline farmers everywhere use seaweed for fertilizer. Irish moss is used to thicken puddings and candies. Laver is prized by the Chinese as an ingredient for soup. Dulse is used for food in Ireland, Scotland, and some parts of the United States. *Gracilaria spinosa* is used for nest-building by a swallow-like Oriental bird. These nests are used to make the famous Chinese bird's-nest soup.

If you would like to try seaweed in cooking, too, look for some sea lettuce. It is easy to recognize because it looks just like limp leaves of salad lettuce and it is a brilliant green color. Shred some of it very fine (since it is rather tough and chewy) and add it to a salad. It won't change the *taste* of the salad very much, but the spectacular color will make one of the prettiest dishes you have ever seen.

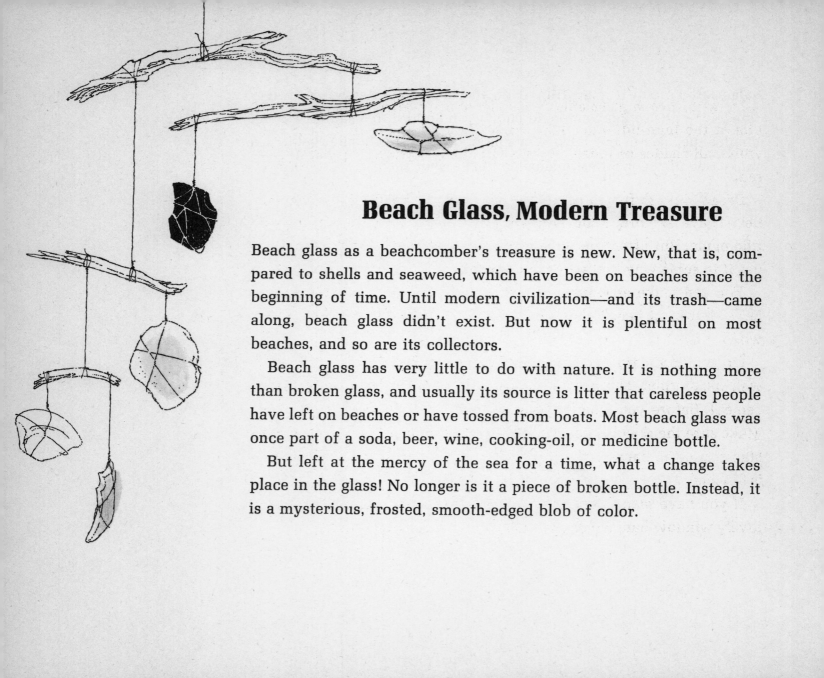

Beach Glass, Modern Treasure

Beach glass as a beachcomber's treasure is new. New, that is, compared to shells and seaweed, which have been on beaches since the beginning of time. Until modern civilization—and its trash—came along, beach glass didn't exist. But now it is plentiful on most beaches, and so are its collectors.

Beach glass has very little to do with nature. It is nothing more than broken glass, and usually its source is litter that careless people have left on beaches or have tossed from boats. Most beach glass was once part of a soda, beer, wine, cooking-oil, or medicine bottle.

But left at the mercy of the sea for a time, what a change takes place in the glass! No longer is it a piece of broken bottle. Instead, it is a mysterious, frosted, smooth-edged blob of color.

Look for beach glass among the shells or pebbles or in the rubble pile at the high-tide line. You will find that it most often comes in white, all shades of green, amber, blue, and—treasure of treasures— red.

Beach glass is fun to collect just because it is so pretty. And you never have to worry about preparing it properly or learning its scientific name. But after you have a sizable collection, you may want to use it in some way that will show it off.

You can make an unusual mobile by fastening fine wires around large chunks of beach glass and hanging them on threads from driftwood sticks.

Or you might try arranging the glass on a driftwood board for a wall decoration. The beach glass is held in place with clear epoxy cement. Before you glue the glass, wash it in fresh water and dry it. Make sure the wood is perfectly dry. Put a small screw eye or a large staple into the back of the wood so that you can hang it up when it is finished.

If you have many very tiny chips of beach glass, you can make a lovely window hanging or a Christmas tree ornament.

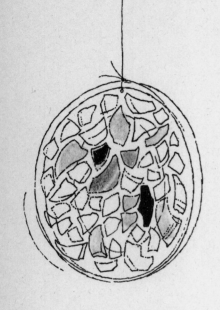

WINDOW ORNAMENT

You will need: **Beach-glass chips**
A clear plastic cover from a coffee can or
other container
Clear epoxy cement
Tweezers
A toothpick

Punch a small hole near one edge of the plastic cover so that you will be able to hang it. With the rim side up, mix epoxy cement right on the plastic. Spread it evenly over the surface with the toothpick. Drop on the glass chips with tweezers so that you don't get your fingers in the glue. Allow to dry thoroughly.

These disks look as lovely as stained glass when hung in a sunny window. And they are perfect for window walls or glass doors where you need something to show that it *is* glass and not to be walked through.

If you want to use the disks for Christmas tree ornaments, you might like to vary the shapes. Before you do anything else, trace a star, a bird, an angel, or any other simple shape onto the plastic with a crayon. Cut out the shape with scissors, punch a hole at the top, and proceed as before. One word of caution: You really must use small glass chips. Large pieces of glass will not stay glued to the flexible plastic.

Use your larger pieces of beach glass to make a decorative hot plate.

HOT PLATE

You will need: **Beach glass**
A package of plaster of paris
A small pie pan (metal, glass, or foil)
An empty coffee can for mixing plaster
A stirring stick
A spoonful of cooking oil
Felt or flannel
Glue

Select pieces of beach glass of contrasting colors, about enough to cover the surface of the pie pan.

Read the mixing directions on the package of plaster of paris. Add plaster to water in an empty can and stir until it is smooth. It should be a little thicker than coffee cream.

Grease the pie pan lightly with the oil and pour in the mixed plaster until the pan is about three-quarters full. The plaster should be at least a half-inch deep. Arrange the glass on top of the plaster in any pattern you like. Press in thick or curved pieces so that you have a flat surface. Try to work fairly quickly, as the plaster sets in a few minutes. You will notice that the plaster gets hot as it sets.

When the plaster is hard, carefully turn the pan over on the table and tap the bottom gently. When the hot plate comes out, it may still be damp. Let it stand overnight or until it is completely dry. Then glue felt, flannel, or other soft material on the bottom so that the hot plate won't mar the table.

Coral, Wood, and Other Surprises

If you live in a tropical climate near a coral beach, you have a beach-combers' paradise. Staghorn, brain, star, and leaf are all common varieties of white coral. They are so lovely that they can be used as decorative objects as is. Coral is most common on the south Atlantic and Gulf coasts, but there are a few Pacific varieties, too. One of these, *Balanophylla,* is orange in color.

Put a few branches of staghorn coral in with the flowers when you make a table centerpiece. Or put the flowers into a low bowl, stand the bowl on a plate or tray, and place a border of coral chunks around it. Make coral sculpture by using your imagination and the directions for pebble sculpture.

There is one coral, *Astrangia danae,* that lives along the Atlantic

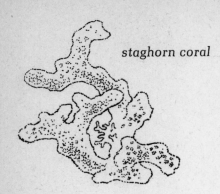

staghorn coral

astrangia

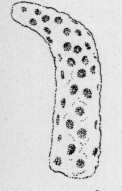

eyed coral

Coast as far north as Cape Cod. It is usually found in small white patches attached to rocks. Sometimes it is flat with a starlike pattern; sometimes it grows in branches.

If you find a bit of *Astrangia danae*, take it home in a container of sea water. Change the water often and the coral will remain alive for a number of days. Look at it every day with a magnifying glass and watch the changes that take place as the coral grows. You will see the living animals, the *polyps,* inside the little cups that house them. Coral is the skeleton of the polyp. The entire colony of polyps keeps forming new coral at the bottoms of the cups. The polyps, in turn, are pushed outward so that they are always near the surface. The coral continues to grow as long as the polyps remain alive. It stays behind long after the polyps have died and disappeared. Many islands and the reefs around them are formed entirely of coral.

Another beachcomber's favorite that was once alive is driftwood. Driftwood is found on most ocean beaches, as well as on the shores of lakes. A famous source for driftwood is Olympic State Park in the state of Washington, where the beaches are literally covered with it. But this is not the case in many places. Driftwood is so sought after

on some beaches that you have to get up at the crack of dawn to beat the rush if you want any large pieces.

Large doesn't mean *huge*. At least once, every eager beachcomber goes charging up to a great prize chunk of driftwood only to find out that he can't budge it without the aid of a derrick. And then there are the smallish ones that seem to have been covered over with a bit of sand. You start to scoop away the sand—and you scoop and you scoop and you dig and you dig. It finally dawns on you that the little log you saw is really the smallest branch of a giant tree. And it's still attached!

One of the things that make driftwood so fascinating is that it is often a ready-made sculpture when you find it. Twisted and tortured by wind, sun, and water, driftwood takes exotic and beautiful forms. Sometimes its art form is abstract; sometimes it takes the shape of a fish, a bird, or an animal.

Driftwood boards are perfect for name signs in front of a beach house and as bases for paintings, mosaics, or collages of all kinds. There is no more suitable background for mounting shells.

BEACHCOMBER'S COLLAGE

You will need: **A large flat piece of driftwood**
OR any large board and many small flat bits
  of driftwood
Shells
Dried seaweed, beach grass, pebbles, sand,
  feathers, reeds, or anything at all from
  the beach
Clear epoxy cement
Clear household cement

This one is a real free-for-all because it depends on what you have. Mount your specimens directly on a driftwood board. You might try a whole beach scene, using sand, pebbles, shells, and plants.

If you don't have a driftwood board, use any kind of board or a piece of plywood. Mount your specimens on easy-to-find small pieces of driftwood and then glue them onto the big backing. Use the household cement for attaching delicate plants and feathers.

Driftwood can make a lovely holder for a bowl of flowers or a pot of ivy. Often there is a hole in the wood that is large enough to hold a slender container such as an olive jar. If you use the driftwood outdoors, you can just fill the hole with earth and plant right in it.

If you find a large piece of driftwood with a graceful shape, you may want to try making a driftwood lamp. The wire runs through a piece of pipe which fits into a hole drilled in the wood. If you are not

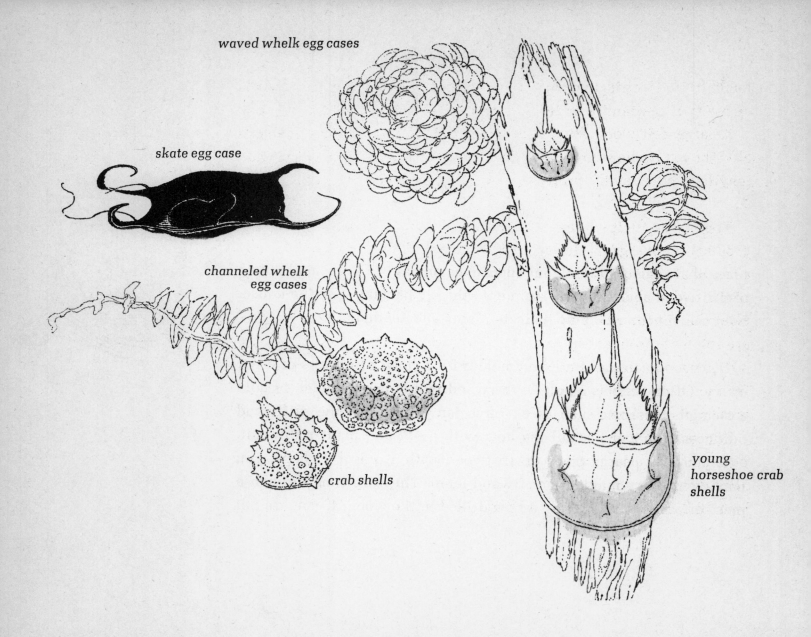

waved whelk egg cases

skate egg case

channeled whelk
egg cases

crab shells

young
horseshoe crab
shells

handy with electrical wiring, you may need some help from an adult member of the family or from your local hardware store.

A large driftwood stump makes a marvelous coffee table base. Saw the top of the stump flat and add a top of heavy glass. Again, this may best be a family project.

There is no limit to what the sea tosses up. Both skates and whelks produce their eggs in sturdy cases which are often found in abundance. Skate egg cases look like stiff black won-tons with long trailing corners. The channeled whelk lays eggs in flat parchment-like cases all strung together on a parchment string. The waved-whelk egg cases are small and round, but they are joined together to make a light-as-air sphere the size and color of a tennis ball. They are all fair game for the beachcomber. So are common crab shells, discarded shells of growing horseshoe crabs, or objects that are covered with barnacles.

Barnacles are the familiar animals that attach themselves to the bottoms of ships and to wharves, piers, and pilings. When they are alive, they look something like molar teeth. When they are dead, they look like molars with holes in them.

Barnacle-covered stones or shells are often quite beautiful and make lovely gifts. Since they are usually dingy when found, soak them overnight in a pail of water with one cup of bleach added. When the barnacles are snowy white, rinse them in fresh water. They make charming holders for tiny dried flowers and are a smash hit aglow with birthday candles.

If you beachcomb on the Northwest coast, you have the special thrill of hunting for agates, jaspers, and other gem stones that are washed down to the beach by the rivers.

The best thing about beachcombing, of course, is that you never know what you will find. Every wave brings a new supply of treasure. Among the objects I have found on the beach is a glass insulator from a telephone pole. The pale green glass is neither broken nor chipped, just beautifully frosted by the action of the sea. It makes a fine paperweight. I also found a heavy brass oarlock (the remains of an unlucky fisherman's boat?), now another paperweight. The incoming tide has provided me with a perfectly good clam rake, a large fishing net, and several traps of various shapes and sizes.

Some things travel long distances. Green glass floats wrapped in netting sometimes break loose from Japanese fishermen's nets and drift to our Pacific shores. And a friend made a really exciting find— a sealed bottle with a note inside that had come all the way across the Atlantic from Ireland!

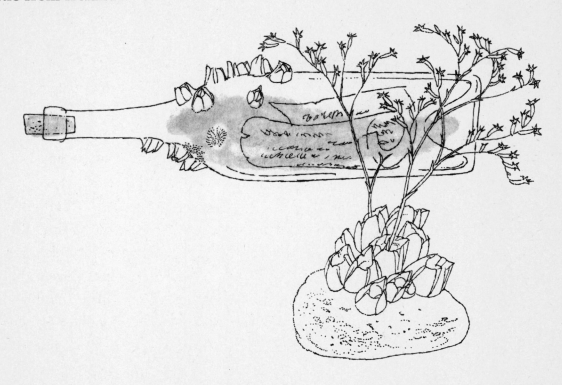

Save for a Rainy Day

Every summer at the beach has its share of rainy days. No serious beachcomber is kept off the beach by a little rain. On the other hand, he doesn't want to stay out there all day and get soaked, either.

You can have your own miniature beach at home if you prepare for it in advance. Keep your eyes open for a fish tank that isn't in use, a very large glass bowl, or even a wide-mouthed jar. The fish tank is best if you can get a salt-water tank. The sea water will corrode a tank with metal parts.

When that rainy day comes along, take a plastic pail and go to the beach. Scoop up some of the sea bottom—sand, mud, or whatever it is. Put it into your pail and add sea water. Then go on a hunt for anything alive. Collect snails, clams, mole crabs, small jellyfish, several

different kinds of seaweed, even a small fish if you can catch one in a net. It is important to take everything from the same area. A mud snail will not live in sand and a crab will not live in mud.

Take your catch home quickly and make your own small sea community in a tank (or bowl, jar, or dishpan).

Copy the natural conditions as exactly as you can. Put the bottom material on the bottom and bank it up on one side to make a "beach" that is above the water line. Add the seaweed, the water, and any animals that you have. Be sure to use only water that came from the original place. Add a little every day. It may contain microscopic food for your animals to eat. They may also get some food (as well as oxygen) from the living seaweed. If you have a fish or a couple of shellfish, you can add a small pinch of fish food or a crumb of bread or meat to the tank every day. Too much food will decay and spoil the water.

Examine the contents of the tank with a magnifying glass. You will probably see many things that are hidden from the naked eye.

If you are lucky, you may be able to keep the contents of your tank alive for a long time. Don't feel too disappointed if you don't succeed, because even professional oceanographers sometimes have a great deal of trouble with a sea tank. On the other hand, I have known children who kept one going most of a summer.

If it's still raining and you need another activity, make a plaster model of a fish. A fish you have caught, preferably.

FISH MODEL

You will need: **The fish**
An empty shoebox (or any box slightly larger
and deeper than the fish)
A couple of pounds of modeling clay that
stays soft (Play-Doh works well)
Plaster of paris and a can to mix it in
A stirring stick
Watercolors or model paints
A watercolor brush
A paper clip

Any time that you go fishing in either salt water or fresh water, pick out your rainy-day fish and put it in the freezer. Don't clean it or do anything else to it; just put it in a plastic bag. Leave it in the freezer until you are ready to make the model.

Knead the clay until it is soft and put a thick smooth layer—thicker than the fish—in the bottom of the box. Take the frozen fish out of the bag and press it hard into the clay. The fish should be half buried in clay, but make sure you don't push it through to the box. Now lift out the fish carefully so that you leave a perfect impression in the clay. If it isn't perfect, flatten out the clay and start over. Be sure the clay around the fish impression is smooth and even. When you are finished, put the fish back in the freezer.

Now mix the plaster according to directions until it is a little thicker than coffee cream. Pour it slowly and carefully into the fish mold, filling every tiny groove. Keep pouring, all around the sides, until the plaster is at least a half-inch thick. Make a hook out of a straightened paper clip and stick the end into the plaster at the right spot for hanging.

When the plaster is thoroughly hard and dry, peel away the box and then the clay. Save the clay to use over again. It may smell a little fishy, so don't mix it with other clay.

Take the poor fish out of the freezer once more and use it as a model while you paint your plaster model the same colors. You can also paint on a label telling the name of the fish, when you caught it, and its weight if you like.

If you do a lot of fishing, you can make a whole collection of models of different kinds of fish.

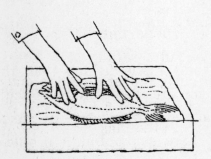

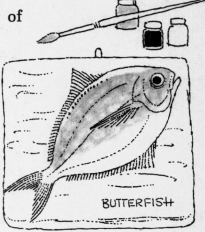

BUTTERFISH

The Beachcomber's Cookbook

All beachcombers, like all people, like to eat. And an expert beach-comber knows how to find the makings for a fabulous meal right on the beach—and how to cook the meal as well.

Shellfish are easy to find on most beaches and easy to cook, too. The best time to go shellfishing is at low tide. Daily newspapers usually give the times of high tide. Most commonly (but not every place) there are high tides twice a day and a low tide follows a high tide by about six and a quarter hours.

In many areas, bay beaches are better for shellfishing than the ocean beach, but this depends on where you are. The delicious Pacific razor clam is found only on the ocean beach. Before you set out, check the local health department to make sure there is no pollution problem in the waters where you will be shellfishing.

If it isn't too cold and there is nothing sharp underfoot, go collecting in your bare feet. Otherwise wear boots or sneakers. You may have to wade out about knee-deep. A clam rake may be useful, a small trowel is always useful, and so is a pail for your haul. In cool weather, rubber gloves will help to keep your hands from freezing. And don't forget to get a shellfish license if the local laws call for it. At the same time, find out the regulations covering how many and what size of each shellfish may be taken.

There are a number of varieties of clams along both the Atlantic and Pacific coasts. Hard-shell clams can be eaten raw if they are small. The very large ones are often best cooked in chowder.

You usually have to wade for hard-shells. They aren't deeply buried, so if you are barefoot, use your toes to feel for them. You will learn to recognize a clam shell under your toes in no time at all. When you feel one, use your hands to pick it up.

If you don't want to use your feet or if you are wearing boots, dig in with the clam rake and lift it up. Water and sand flow through the tines, and the clams are left behind. In most places, the rakes are made so that illegally small clams will fall through, too. If you do not use a rake, be sure to throw back undersized clams so that they will have a chance to grow and breed.

Soft-shell clams, which are marvelous steamed, are found just at the water line. These are apt to be buried more deeply than their hard-shell relatives, so you have to start by digging a hole. To find a good spot, look for little holes in the wet sand. If you see small jets of water popping out of the holes, you are definitely in the right place.

Use your trowel to make a hole about six inches deep. After that, it is best to use your hands because the soft shells are very thin and crush easily. The first thing you see when you find a clam is its long neck (the siphon), which looks like a big thick worm. It will draw back as soon as it is exposed, but keep digging and follow it to the shell. Dig out the clam carefully with your fingers, rinse it off, and put it in the pail. Clams close their shells when handled. If one remains open and doesn't close when you poke it, the clam is dead and must be discarded. When you have enough (at least a dozen per person), you are ready to make steamed clams.

hard-shell clam

STEAMED CLAMS

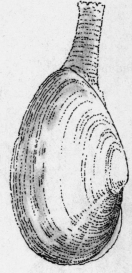

soft-shell clam

Scrub the clams well with a brush and put them into a large bowl of fresh water. Leave them in the refrigerator for one hour or more so that they rid themselves of sand.

After soaking, dump the clams into the sink and rinse them again. Now put them into a large kettle with a cup of water. Cover the kettle and let it steam until all the shells have opened—about five to fifteen minutes depending on the kind of clams. As soon as all the clams are open, remove them from the stove. Serve each portion of clams with a small bowl of melted butter and a bowl of the broth from the bottom of the kettle.

Steamed clams are strictly finger food, so don't worry about your manners. Lift up a clam by its neck, rinse it off in the broth, dip it in the melted butter, and bite it off just at the base of the neck. You can eat the necks, too, but, they are usually very tough.

71

Mussels, a highly prized food in Europe, are not as often appreciated here. They should be, because they are plentiful everywhere and they are delicious.

Look for mussels attached to rocks or pilings. They are lumped together in great clusters and are firmly attached by their own *byssus* threads. Make sure they are alive, which means that their shells are tightly closed. Pull or cut them off and get ready to make sailor's mussels, or what the French call *moules à la marinière*.

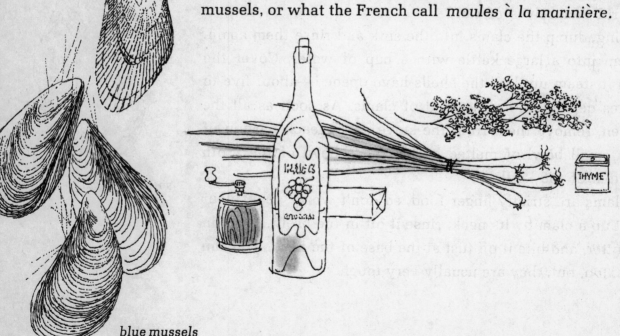

ribbed mussel

blue mussels

MOULES A LA MARINIERE

The worst part of preparing mussels is cleaning them. You have to get off all the threads, seaweed, barnacles, and other odds and ends that are attached to the shells. The easiest way to do this is to use a stiff wire brush. It is a good idea to wear work gloves to protect your fingers.

For three or four people, prepare about three dozen mussels. When the mussels are thoroughly clean, put them in fresh water in the refrigerator for an hour or two. At cooking time, rinse the mussels again and put them into a large kettle with:

> **1 cup water or dry white wine**
> **1/4 cup chopped shallots, onions, or scallions**
> **4 large sprigs of parsley**
> **A dash of pepper**
> **A pinch of thyme**
> **1/2 stick (4 tablespoons) butter**

Cover and steam until the shells are all open, which should take about five minutes. Serve in large soup plates with a portion of the broth and a sprinkle of chopped parsley. With a green salad (made

with sea lettuce, of course) and hot French bread and butter, this is a true gourmet meal.

The only one that is better is that greatest of beach events, a clambake.

A CLAMBAKE

You will need: **A washtub, clam boiler, or large enamel pot
with cover
Lots of seaweed
1 quart of fresh water
8 baking potatoes, scrubbed and wrapped in foil
4 chickens cut up, each portion wrapped in cheesecloth
8 one-pound lobsters
8 ears of corn, husked and wrapped in foil
Plenty of steamer clams
Melted butter
Salt and pepper**

You can have your clambake on the beach over a charcoal grill; or, if you prefer, you can cook it at home on the stove. The quantities given are for eight people, but the amounts can be increased or decreased. The only limit is the size of your pot.

First dig the clams, scrub them well with a brush, and let them soak in a bowl or pail of fresh water for at least an hour. Rinse the seaweed several times; then soak it for about forty-five minutes in fresh water to get rid of sand. Prepare the rest of the ingredients.

Now line the bottom of the pot with a four-inch layer of wet seaweed. Add the water and put the pot over high heat. When the water boils, add the potatoes and more seaweed. Cover and cook over lower heat for fifteen minutes.

Add the chicken pieces and a layer of seaweed. Cover and cook fifteen minutes more.

Add the lobsters and more seaweed. Cover and cook eight minutes.

Add the foil-wrapped corn, cover, and cook ten minutes.

Add the clams. Cover and steam until the clams open—from five to ten minutes.

The total cooking time is about one hour. Now take out just enough food for the first round, keeping the rest hot in the pot. Use clam shells for your melted butter and dunk everything in it.

Eat until you are stuffed, wash your hands in the sea, and take a nap. You earned it!

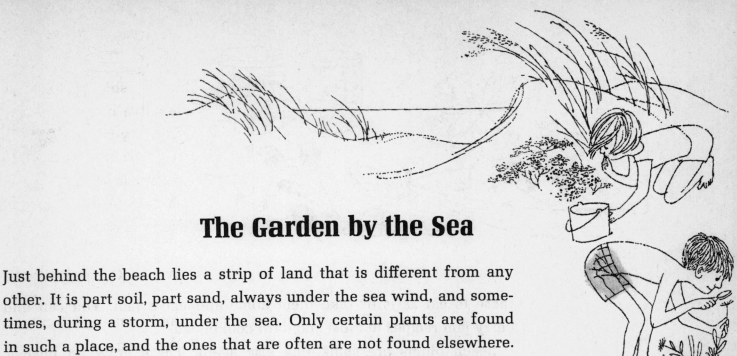

The Garden by the Sea

Just behind the beach lies a strip of land that is different from any other. It is part soil, part sand, always under the sea wind, and sometimes, during a storm, under the sea. Only certain plants are found in such a place, and the ones that are often are not found elsewhere.

Everyone notices the showy palms of the South and West coasts, and the masses of colorful wild flowers in all coastal areas. But there are many plants in the seaside garden that are hardly noticed at all except by the beachcomber.

Sand strawberries and sand blackberries grow in profusion, but they hug the ground and are easy to overlook. Blueberries grow on bushes, but the berries are often hidden in the leaves. Pick any of

these to eat as is or take them home and make jam. You can find berry jam recipes in most standard cookbooks.

Beach plums are something else again. These grow on bushes, ripen at summer's end, and look like purple cherries. They are found along the Atlantic coast and around the Great Lakes. People notice beach plums but can't figure out what to do with them. They are too sour to eat raw. The seeds are so large that it seems difficult to pit them for cooking. And most cookbooks are of no help. But you can make excellent beach plum jam.

BEACH PLUM JAM

You will need: **Beach plums**
Strainer
Large kettle
Sugar
Measuring cup
Large cooking spoon
Sterilized (boiled) jelly jars with tops
Labels

beach plums

Wash the fruit, pick off the stems, and place the plums in a large kettle. Barely cover the fruit with water and cook until it is mushy. Force the mush through a coarse strainer and measure it. For every cupful of fruit add one cup of sugar. Put all this into the kettle and boil, stirring frequently. When the mixture is thick and clear, start to test it. It is done when a little of it hangs from the edge of the spoon in two wide drops that run together into one drop before it falls from the spoon.

Pour the jam into jars that have been sterilized by boiling, and seal. When cool, label.

79

bayberry

Another shrub of the East coast is bayberry. Its narrow leaves are excellent to use in cooking in place of bay leaves, especially in fish dishes. In the fall, the bayberry bush is covered with clusters of the tiny, gray, waxy berries that are used to make bayberry candles. These make splendid Christmas gifts.

Although the history books tell us how the American colonists made their candles of bayberries, the books seem to leave out something. Or the colonists knew something that nobody knows any more. I have tried to follow the so-called colonial method and found that a large pailful of berries (the fruit of hours of picking while battling hot sun, gnats, mosquitoes, brambles, and poison ivy) yielded about enough wax to seal a letter! It must take tons of berries to make one candle.

But since we have conveniences the colonists didn't have, there is a way around the problem. Although bayberries aren't as rich in wax as we have been led to believe, they are positively bursting with fragrance. A little goes a long way, so if you supply your own wax, you can make candles that smell like the real thing when they burn.

BAYBERRY CANDLES

You will need: **Bayberries (as many as possible—at least a couple of quarts)**
A kettle
A tall (46 oz.) empty juice can
A strainer
Several cheap, tall candles
A pencil or stick

Put the bayberries into the kettle, cover them with water, and boil for about fifteen minutes. Strain the liquid, cool it, and put it in the refrigerator until the wax settles in a hard cake on top. Keep the wax and throw away the rest (the water and berries).

Put the candles into the juice can, stand the can in a pot of water, and heat it slowly until the wax melts.

Pick out the wicks with a pencil or a stick so that you can re-use them. Plain string won't work as well. Break up the bayberry wax and melt it into the candle wax.

Make a short candle first because it is easier. To dip a candle, hold a wick by one end and dip it into the wax. Pull it out and hold it over the can to drip while the wax sets. Be sure to wait until

the wax is firm. If necessary, straighten it. Then dip again. Keep dipping until the candle is as fat as you want it to be. When it is finished, trim off the end of the wick if it is too long. Don't expect your candle to look like a bought one. It should have a handmade look that may be somewhat uneven.

Dipping candles takes time and patience. You might find it easier to use a milk carton as a mold to make a larger candle that is square in shape. First, save and wash out an empty milk carton and cut off its top. Pour the wax into the carton, as high as you want your candle to be. Remember, though, that your wick should be an inch or two longer than the height of your candle. Now drop one end of the wick into the center of the candle all the way to the bottom, and hold it in place by wrapping the other end around a stick or pencil resting across the top of the carton. Let the wax set until it is firm, then peel away the carton and trim the wick to the proper length.

You won't find bayberries on the Pacific coast, but you will find sea-figs. These are a delicious fruit. Beach peas (found on both coasts) bear lovely sweet-pea-like flowers in the spring. Later in the summer, pick the peas. They look like farm peas except that they are much smaller. And they taste better. Cook beach peas like regular peas or eat them raw.

In many areas, the end of summer means the end of beach weather. Unless you live where it is warm the year round, make some preparations for the cold season.

Seaside lavender and seaside goldenrod make fine winter bou-

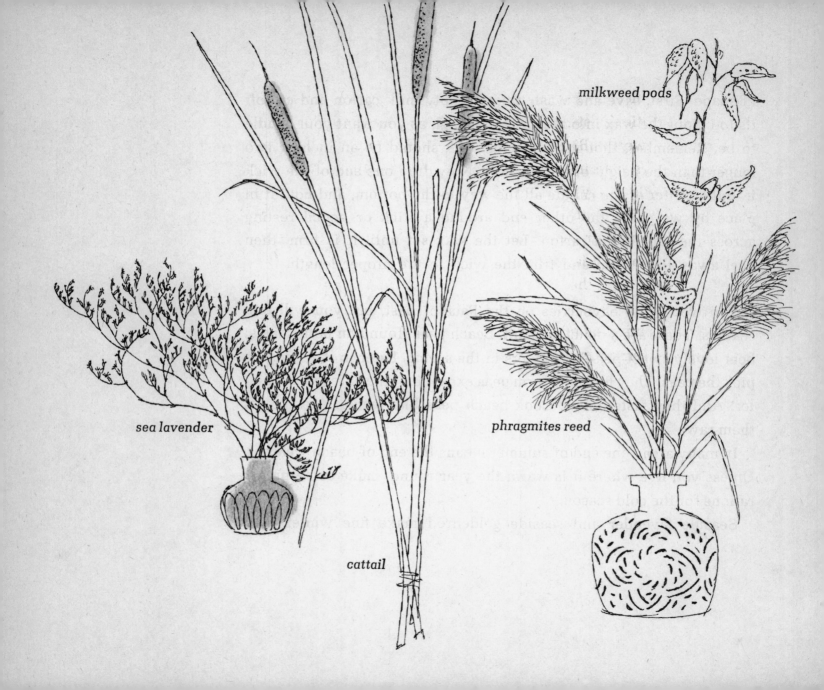

milkweed pods

sea lavender

cattail

phragmites reed

quets. Pick the flowers in the fall, put them into a shopping bag upside down, and tie the stems to the handle. Put the bag in a dry place for about two weeks. Bittersweet (*Celastrus scandens*, whose small greenish flowers turn into red and yellow fruits), thistle, milkweed pods, and cattails all dry well. Feathery reeds can be picked all fall and winter and used just as they are.

For the beachcomber, a summer at the beach can last all year long. Every time you open a jar of beachcomber's jam, you can almost feel the salt breeze and the sunshine. The winter bouquets, holiday candles, the sculptures, shell beads, and other works of art that you made are all reminders of the summer's joy. And even more important, they are reminders that another summer is on its way.

Some Common Shells and Seaweeds

Illustrations by Laurel Brown

The following pages will help you to identify the shells and seaweeds that you find, by showing some of the most common species in your section of the country. They are not, however, intended to take the place of complete field guides. You may never find some of the specimens that are shown, and you may find many that are not included here at all.

The bibliography at the end of this book suggests other books that will help you to identify all the things you find, and your librarian can suggest many more. They will help you to become an even better beachcomber than you already are.

SOME COMMON SHELLS OF THE ATLANTIC AND GULF COASTS

Turkey Wing
Arca occidentalis
North Carolina to Florida

Hard-shell or Quahog Clam
Venus mercenaria
Maine to Florida

Atlantic Surf Clam
Spisula solidissima
Labrador to North Carolina

Rose Petal Tellin
Tellina lineata
North Carolina to Florida

Coquina
Donax variabilis
North Carolina to Texas

Elegant Dosinia
Dosinia elegans
North Carolina to Florida

Razor or Jackknife Clam
Ensis directus
Maine to Florida

China Cockle
Trachycardium egmontianum
New Jersey to Florida

Blue Mussel
Mytilus edulis
Maine to Florida

Virginia Oyster
Ostrea virginica
Nova Scotia to Florida

Jingle Shell
Anomia simplex
Maine to Florida

Atlantic Bay Scallop
Pecten irradians
Maine to North Carolina

Calico Scallop
Pecten gibbus
North Carolina to Florida

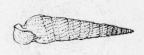
Atlantic Auger
Terebra dislocata
Virginia to Texas

Boat or Slipper Shell
Crepidula fornicata
Nova Scotia to Texas

Florida Fighting Conch
Strombus alatus
Florida

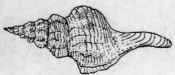

Florida Horse Conch
Fasciolaria gigantea
North Carolina to Florida

Alphabet Cone
Conus spurius atlanticus
Florida

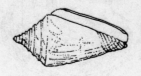

Florida Cone
Conus floridanus
North Carolina to Florida

Measled Cowry
Cypraea exanthema
North Carolina to Florida

Atlantic Plate Limpet
Acmaea testudinalis
Labrador to Connecticut

Northern Moon Snail
Polinices heros
Maine to New Jersey

Apple Murex
Murex pomum
North Carolina to Florida

Oyster Drill
Urosalpinx cinerea
Maine to Florida

Lettered Olive
Oliva sayana
North Carolina to Texas

Common Periwinkle
Littorina littorea
Nova Scotia to New Jersey

Common Atlantic Sundial
Architectonica granulata
North Carolina to Florida

Banded Tulip Shell
Fasciolaria distans
North Carolina to Texas

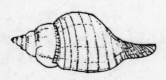

New England Neptune
Neptunea decemcostata
Nova Scotia to Massachusetts

Channeled Whelk
Busycon canaliculatum
Massachusetts to Texas

SOME COMMON SHELLS OF THE PACIFIC COAST

Little Ark
Acar pernoides
Santa Monica, Calif. south

Button Shell
Glycymeris subobsoleta
Alaska to California

Rock Venus
Protothaca staminea
Alaska to California

Alaska Surf Clam
Spisula alaskana
Alaska to Puget Sound

California Wedge
Donax californica
Santa Barbara, Calif. south

Blunt Razor Clam
Solen sicarius
Vancouver Island to Calif.

Nuttall's Cockle
Clinocardium nuttallii
Alaska to San Diego, Calif.

California Mussel
Mytilus californicus
Alaska to California

Native Pacific Oyster
Ostrea lurida
Washington to California

Jingle Shell
Anomia peruviana
San Pedro, Calif. south

   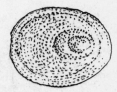

Pink Scallop
Chlamys hericus
Alaska to San Diego, Calif.

Black Abalone
Haliotis cracherodii
Oregon to California

California Cone
Conus californicus
San Francisco, Calif. south

File Limpet
Acmaea limatula
Washington to California

Keyhole Limpet
Fissurella volcano
Monterey, Calif. south

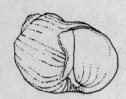

Lewis's Moon Snail
Polinices lewisii
British Columbia to Calif.

Purple Olive
Olivella biplicata
Monterey to San Diego, Calif.

Sculptured Rock Shell
Ocenebra interfossa
Alaska to California

Channeled Top
Calliostoma doliarius
Alaska to San Diego, Calif.

Black Turban
Tegula funebralis
British Columbia to Calif.

SOME COMMON SHELLS OF HAWAII

Hawaiian Cockle
Trachycardium hawaiensis

Little Pearl Oyster
Pteria nebulosa

Painted Auger
Terebra strigillata

Spotted Conch
Strombus maculatus

Striate Cone
Conus striatus
(very poisonous!)

Ringed Cowrie
Cypraea annulata

Horned Helmet
Cassis Cornuta

Common Nerite
Nerita picea

Hawaiian Top
Trochus sandwichensis

White Wentletrap
Epitonium decussata

SOME COMMON SEAWEEDS

GREEN

Acetabularia (Mermaid's Cup)
South Atlantic and Gulf of Mexico

Bryopsis (Sea Moss)
Atlantic and Pacific

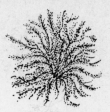

Cladophora
North Atlantic

Codium (Sponge Seaweed)
South Atlantic, Gulf, and Pacific

Enteromorpha
Atlantic, Gulf and Pacific

Penicillus (Merman's Shaving Brush)
South Atlantic and Gulf of Mexico

Ulva (Sea Lettuce)
Atlantic, Gulf, and Pacific

BROWN (often olive-green)

Agarum (Sea Colander)
North Atlantic

Alaria
North Atlantic

Chorda
Northern shores

Laminaria
Northern shores

Fucus (Rockweed)
Northern shores

Macrocystis (Giant Kelp)
Pacific

Nereocystis (**Ribbon** Kelp)
Pacific

Sargassum
Atlantic, Gulf, and Pacific

Chondrus (Irish Moss)
North Atlantic

Corallina
North Atlantic

Dasya
Atlantic and Pacific

Delesseria
North Atlantic

Gelidium
Atlantic and Pacific

Grinnellia
Cape Cod south

Ptilota (Featherweed)
North Atlantic and Pacific

Porphyra (Laver)
Atlantic, Gulf, and Pacific

Polysiphonia
Atlantic and Pacific

Rhodymenia (Dulse)
North Atlantic and Pacific

BIBLIOGRAPHY

ARNOLD, Augusta Foote, *The Sea-Beach at Ebb-Tide*, paper ed. New York: Dover Publications, Inc., 1949.

CARSON, Rachel, *The Edge of the Sea*, paper ed. New York: New American Library, Inc., 1959.

COOPER, Elizabeth K., *Science on the Shores and Banks*, paper ed. New York: Harcourt, Brace and World, Inc., 1960.

MORRIS, Percy A., *A Field Guide to the Shells of Our Atlantic and Gulf Coasts*. The Peterson Field Guide Series. Boston: Houghton Mifflin Company, 1951.

MORRIS, Percy A., *A Field Guide to Shells of the Pacific Coast and Hawaii*. The Peterson Field Guide Series. Boston: Houghton Mifflin Company, 1966.

STERLING, Dorothy, *The Outer Lands: A Natural History Guide to Cape Cod, Martha's Vineyard, Nantucket, Block Island and Long Island*. Garden City, N.Y.: Natural History Press, 1967.

SUNSET MAGAZINE EDITORIAL STAFF, *Sunset Beachcombers' Guide to the Pacific Coast*, paper ed. Menlo Park, Calif.: Lane, 1967.

YONGE, Charles M. *The Sea Shore*, paper ed. New York: Atheneum Publishers, 1963.

INDEX